The Shadow Work Trap

The Shadow Work Trap

How It Hijacks Your Spiritual Awakening And
What to Do Instead

by

Queen Heterodoxika

The Shadow Work Trap: How It Hijacks Your Spiritual
Awakening And What to Do Instead
By Queen Heterodoxika

First published in the United States of America in 2025
By Living As God, LLC

For information, write Living As God, LLC, Five Greentree
Centre, Suite 104, 525 Route 73 North, Marlton, NJ 08053

ISBN 979-8-9929871-0-2

Also by the Author

Spiritual Lies You've Been Told (Releasing Fall 2025)

To Bob who believed for, and before, me.

To Susan who saw my potential and took a risk to show it to me.

Thank you for showing me the truly transformative power of caring about another person.

CONTENTS

INTRODUCTION

If you have found this book, there is still time. The codes embedded in this textbook will unlock what is necessary for you to begin. What you contain is meant to be shared with the world to help uplift humanity and make great contributions to an ascending world.

I have published this book while my community is in development because I have been instructed to produce a semi-solitary path as soon as possible. There are missions that have not been fulfilled. Events are unfolding faster than many can adapt. Help is needed now. I prefer to work with people directly because transmission is part of my work. Nuances can be difficult to discern in daily life so access to a seer is helpful while learning. Having someone with advanced psychic skills help you through something can be invaluable in real time. This will be a beginning and you can join us later. Start with what you can do with the program in this book now.

I work with two types of spiritual seekers. The majority are survivors of severe trauma, abuse and neglect and a smaller group who experience fringe metaphysical phenomena - bilocation, spontaneous, disruptive awakenings, living on prana, etc. Sometimes these groups overlap. I have extensive lived experience with both. This book is focused on severe trauma, abuse and neglect survivors in the spiritual awakening community. If you had a fairly happy childhood and want to learn manifesting, find another book. I love you and there's nothing here for you.

Survivors of severe trauma and abuse are the most potentially powerful beings on the planet. You are. This is due to several reasons. First, as a survivor you have intently searched for what you needed to be supported and how you wanted love to show up for you. You carry the true vision of what love can do here precisely because you know the depths of what the lack of love does. Second, you have discovered and are creating what family, friendships and love of another genuinely are because you needed to create these relationships or may still be searching for these relationships. You needed to search for these relationships because the assigned relationship of parent, sibling, family, trusted friend was violated to such a degree that you have done the difficult sifting through what it means to be a family member or trusted friend and what this role needs to be in your life. You have spent the time creating these roles and that creation time is exclusive to you and enables you to bring more of these roles to fruition. Along these same lines, you had the necessary experiences to force you to go within, where your truth lives, to cultivate internal resources, explore your own psychological makeup, create new ways to cope with your experience and bring forward that which only you can create. It all brought you here.

What you need is in you, not in someone else's teaching. Your life has created a perfect opportunity for you to mine the gold within, to reclaim that which is within you and to search deeper to your true nature so you can bring forward what no one else can bring forward. Your life has been an unlocking process. Being carved so deeply forces the bounce back, the searching for something even higher and fuller which fuels the vision needed to be held to pull in the creations needed.

You've gone down so deep and been hurt so much that the natural bounce your true nature takes gives you a higher vision of what the world can be that needs to be realized. There will be a reclamation of goodness in the world and you will be at the center of it. This is because you can identify and bring forward that good. You are the vision holder if you dare.

Those who did not suffer as much have not yet accessed the same lows. Smaller changes upset them because they have had a more limited experience and no need to access expanded emotion. They have a limited range of life experience which makes it more difficult to access an expanded vision of what can be. They are satisfied with what is. The missions needed to hold the highest vision for the planet and humanity are coming through trauma and abuse survivors. They are needed. What you're not being told is that the visions held by beings here on the planet affect what comes in the future. There's no point waiting around because no one is coming to save us. We're doing it ourselves. We are the boots on the ground. It's why you came here.

The purpose of this book is twofold. First, it is necessary to unlearn the erroneous information you have been told about awakening, develop your personal character and step into your sovereignty. You must embody service to the planet and humanity through supreme accountability for yourself, your actions and your surroundings. This comes as you realize that you don't need to heal forever.

Second, you need to develop a relationship with the energy or consciousness that connects all of creation, seen and unseen. You already have intuition and may have connections to other beings as well. This connection has many benefits for trauma and abuse survivors that are best experienced instead of explained but I will elucidate a relatable aspect to help you understand the approach. They are all enjoyable and healing.

My method is based on dropping prior psychic tools to access information and focusing on developing a connection WITHIN yourself by going through the heart space. This connection to whatever you call this universal energy or consciousness is the main relationship you cultivate. The need for this is twofold. First, most seekers look outside of themselves and do not have an experienced guide to help them understand what they are attempting. This puts you at risk and without finding someone knowledgeable, you may follow a false path and compromise yourself. By going within your heart space searching for your creation point, you eliminate those risks and the psychic development progresses differently than when you start looking outside yourself. This development is the outcome of the second reason.

Trauma and abuse survivors often have a long history of self-help behind them. This can include therapy, psychedelics, religious and spiritual groups, personal development methods and groups and many more. The people I have worked with find that most of these ultimately fail them. They can keep up for awhile but eventually the shine wears off and old habits and feelings return. This is because these methods don't address what you get through my method. Something that should be taught by every awakening being on this planet to as many people as are willing to work with them. That is how to have an intimate and direct connection with your source, your creator, without the need for anyone else. This is the only path to true sovereignty and to knowing truth.

Most of the people I work with did the same things I did when they were going through these self-help options - looking to feel better. As a woman I barely know once said, "Feelings are where you live and the fabric that makes up your world." Trauma and abuse survivors live in vast mental and emotional worlds due to the early need for self-survival and the fact that they lived in a state of nervous system dysregulation. As you probably know, this doesn't resolve itself spontaneously in adulthood without intervention. However, it does begin to resolve through developing a relationship with your source. Nervous system regulation is one of the first steps of your foundation. It's a byproduct of developing this relationship.

The pace of this healing varies by person. It's extremely individual. But the reason it happens is unique and responsible for the activation and cultivation of advanced psychic abilities. The reason all of those programs and groups don't work for trauma and abuse survivors is because most of them are based on discipline and/or vulnerability with someone else. Many survivors carry much shame from childhood which impacts their ability to benefit from these programs and groups. Changing yourself and the way you feel is the primary motivator for staying and trying again. But you cannot discipline yourself from a place of self-recrimination and you cannot discipline yourself enough to make up for an unfulfilled emotional, psychological or neurological need. This may work in the short term but always backfires eventually.

The second reason I teach going within to develop this relationship is because it will provide what nothing else can for you - absolute, unyielding, all-seeing, all-knowing love and unconditional positive regard. I will not say more than that on how the relationship progresses because it's personal to each individual and never what we think it will be. It is always illuminating. Through this relationship, you do not need shadow work because you will be able to have a way to get your own information and a way to know what choices are best for you and a place to go when you need to be filled and so much more. You come to know more about yourself. You grow into the sovereign being you are and don't need others to get spiritual guidance. You become empowered and free. You are not held back by the past anymore. You can live life beyond your wildest dreams and unlock your mission, knowing that you are giving up nothing.

Through developing this relationship, your perception and senses are enhanced and trained in such a way that you are not vulnerable to outside influence and have no need for hearing from other psychics or prophets about what their visions and experiences are. You will have your own font of knowledge within you. You will be able to see through the false light, the fake readers, the opportunists and those pursuing alternate outcomes to your own.

My goal is to have you develop these skills so that you do not need me. In my opinion, that should be the goal of every provider of spiritual or esoteric services on the planet. We should be training others in the methods that we use and how to access what we access so you do not need us and can be sovereign.

But this is not being done. Many secrets are being kept and seekers are going in circles unaware. There are many reasons and this book is not designed to go into all of them. I will mention two of them, however. First, if you teach a man to fish, he no longer goes to the fishmonger to buy fish. He can do it on his own. Second, there is a risk in making some information commonly available. That is why some esoteric information is encoded or given piecemeal and the student must figure out the rest of the clues.

What you will find within this book will enable you to become sovereign if applied in the way it is described. It is a straightforward method and incorporates all the tools I used to become sovereign, communicate with Source and realize my mission.

We need more sovereign beings on the planet, getting their own guidance. You need to be able to receive and follow your own guidance from within no matter what is going on outside. It is only sovereign beings who can carry out the missions that are unlike anything we've seen before on this planet. And what we need is unlike anything seen before on this planet.

You are not meant to be cloistered away, maintaining a high vibration to help the planet. There is something more dynamic, more unique and more exciting in store for you. I know you can feel it. It's why you are here. You know there is more to your life.

You have a mission here. It is unique to you. We need what you have and you are the only one who can do it.

I'm Queen Heterodoxika. It's my job to instruct you on how to heal and discover your mission. I'm sure you've noticed that things are speeding up. We are approaching a very auspicious time and we need all hands on deck, creating what only you can create. We need what you came here to create. Missions are going unfulfilled.

Before you get to work on your mission, you need to discover what it is. The only way to do that is to become the sovereign being you truly are. You need to develop your character, psychic skills and be able to receive advanced spiritual information personalized for you to navigate that path.

You are meant for more. You know it. You can feel it. You've been untangling the wreckage of your past and it's exhausting. That ends now.

My current mission is to assemble this program and make it available to those who are ready. More is coming but start here. I've put the program together here to be accessible on its own until the community is available. I'm making it available to those with unfulfilled missions so everyone who desires it can be activated.

Without discovering your mission, you will never know how amazing life could be. You will not fulfill what you came here to do. There are people who need you. There is a version of you that lives in peace and joy and love each day and wants to be here on the planet helping others and building an amazing life. Your heart knows that and holds the key. You have the opportunity to be a key player in a massive shift for good, unlike anything the cosmos has seen and enjoy doing it.

Ready to get started? The first thing you need to do is drop shadow work. I'll tell you why in the next few pages. The second thing you need to do is make peace with a few unicorns in this book. They are messengers of love, peace, joy and purity. There's no hidden meaning in them. They bring me joy and I love to share joy. We are here for joy!

Part I: Shadow Work Subverts Spiritual Awakening

Shadow Work Ignores Spiritual Causes

The current spiritual community is lying to you. Shadow work is not going to help you advance spiritually. It is not going to help you develop a relationship with Source/God/Love. It will not help you discover your mission. It is a waste of time for those who need to develop advanced skills and bring new frequencies through to share with humanity.

Why is it so commonly suggested?

Because it's the only thing they've got.

Once upon a time someone said that doing shadow work was a good idea. Nobody had a better option so they repeat what they have heard from other people.

But why is shadow work touted as a panacea to what's ailing you? What is the allure?

The purpose is to uncover repressed aspects of your psyche. Then you feel better once you've recognized that the repressed piece is part of you. In practice, this has been helpful to people who are not on a spiritual path.

However, this is a problem if you are on a spiritual path and it is especially damaging for trauma and abuse survivors. Going through a spiritual awakening requires a different modality. Shadow work for awakening people results in frustration, confusion and missing necessary information.

It hijacks your awakening and keeps you trapped in healing loops. Shadow work negates any possible spiritual causes for what you are experiencing. It doesn't say that energetic answers are wrong. It simply has no framework for energy or spirit and denies their existence. It doesn't acknowledge them. So it cannot provide an answer that will be appropriate for someone going through a spiritual awakening who is experiencing phenomena not recognized by the system in which shadow work operates. Shadow work is the hammer and everything looks like a nail.

The main reason shadow work doesn't work for those on a spiritual path can be understood intellectually. The rest are causes which seekers will understand in the next several chapters. But the main reason shadow work doesn't work is due to simple definitions.

Most spiritual paths acknowledge a non-dual ultimate All That Is. It's the idea that we are all one, or we are all love or the Tao, God, Source, etc. You get the idea. If you are All That Is, nothing is outside of you. You encompass everything and everything is you ultimately. Everything is connected. You are the things you like in the world and the things that you don't like. You are the things that you have feelings about one way or the other and the things you have no feelings about. You are all the people doing all those things too. You are everything.

In shadow work, you look at things which are uncomfortable or evoke strong (usually negative) emotions in you. Then you begin to open to the idea, through various methods, that this "triggering" event or person is a repressed aspect of yourself. The goal is to bring that aspect to your conscious awareness so it doesn't prompt the undesired emotional response from you again.

The idea is that relief from this tension is gained through bringing this aspect to light, thus why it is called shadow work. You bring this aspect to light by acknowledging and accepting that it is part of you, not only what you see in someone else. For non-spiritual seekers, this can work well.

However, the issue of seekers beginning to recognize their Divine nature brings conditions which make shadow work ineffective. This issue arises when the seeker begins to realize he or she is a being that encompasses All That Is, not a distinct entity separate from it.

If you are All That Is, nothing is outside of you and you recognize that you are All That Is. If something you experience causes you pain (your "trigger"), you are causing yourself pain which is counterproductive and you would stop immediately unless it had a purpose.

In that instance in which the pain had a purpose, as All That Is, you would know the purpose for the pain since you are All That Is. There would be no confusion over the cause of the pain. Then you would take whatever steps are necessary once the pain had your attention. Thus, the pain is ameliorated. You are able to adjust yourself and your responses accordingly.

Alternatively, you know you are All That Is so there is no need to do shadow work. You already know that everything you encounter is you. Therefore, shadow work has no constructive purpose to you because there is no shadow. All of you would be brought to light by the awareness that you are All That Is. You would be looking at you which you already knew. If Oneness is All There Is, then you are doing this "triggering" activity to yourself. This is what mystics know. You encompass All That Is. I have experienced this along with many of you. You wouldn't have picked up my book if you weren't already on this path.

That is the short answer for why shadow work doesn't work for seekers. If you were operating at the level of Oneness, you wouldn't experience any "trigger" because there would be no unknown aspect of you. How can you be doing this to yourself without your knowledge? If you are going through a spiritual awakening, you need another method to interpret what you are responding to.

First, you need to know some of the problems that happen when you do shadow work on a spiritual path. If you see yourself in any of these, don't worry. I've experienced them all before I identified the lie about shadow work being necessary to awakening.

The system in this book sets you up for success in each of these areas. No matter where you find yourself, it doesn't take long to straighten your course.

The Need for An Expanded Viewpoint, or Shadow Work Operates Only in the Known

One of the ways shadow work derails spiritual seekers is because you are limited by the concepts and knowledge you, or whatever practitioner you're working with, understands or has familiarity with. Therefore, what you can identify as the "trigger" is limited to something you already know. This leaves no room for expansion or growth in new areas or to examine your experience in an alternate light. It limits you to ideas you already understand, have experience with or have heard of. This leads to misidentifying and misunderstanding what you are experiencing while going through a spiritual awakening.

It puts you, specifically your thinking mind, as the most knowledgeable observer of the experience. This is incorrect. You are not your thoughts, your belief systems or your opinions. You are an infinite being having a human experience. It is that perspective which is necessary to embody going through awakening, not the reasoning, analytical mind. You are more than that but more will be revealed as you develop a direct relationship with the Divine to communicate and receive.

Your infinite Source is available to orient you to the nature of your experiences beyond the comprehension of the thinking mind. This is the first intention of awakening beings, to expand consciousness while embodied. You need an expanded view to interpret and understand what you are experiencing. Shadow work has no framework for this and offers no expanded viewpoint. Shadow work makes you look at things you, or whoever you are working with, already know and to choose from that limited knowledge set to determine what the cause of your suffering is. Shadow work doesn't entertain the idea that you could be experiencing something new or novel or an experience designed specifically for you that no one else has a frame of reference for. Shadow work insists that the cause is a known quantity. The danger in this for spiritual seekers is the removal of wonder, exploration and willingness to engage with the unknown for spiritual advancement. It stunts spiritual growth by providing no framework for wonder or discovery of new phenomena. Instead, it sends you down paths that others have already walked, insisting that nothing can be novel, unique or emerging. Sometimes, what you are experiencing is unique to you and necessary for your development only. Doing shadow work prevents these realizations and mistakenly applies the experience to something already known, limiting growth.

Many times during spiritual awakening being upset by something is due to not understanding what you are experiencing and judging it. A better alternative is working with your higher power that has broader knowledge and more advanced understanding than you to help you see what the true message and purpose is behind that experience. This is a path to true expansion.

25

Awakening people doing shadow work are extremely sincere and earnest in their efforts. Unfortunately, the new age culture commonly associated with it has captured the minds of many on this path and instilled a belief that the individual is responsible for everything in their lives. It is an attempt at empowerment.

This is a mis-application of our spiritual nature and does not account for how beings access power in this realm and can affect others. As a result, well-meaning seekers turn things inward, blame themselves and then look for ways to become "better" and different than they are. The self-condemnation is extremely painful and isolating. Seekers then recognize it and do shadow work on that self-condemnation.

The true nature and purpose of the experience is missed because there's no outside input from a higher power with a broader perspective and unconditional positive regard. The cycle continues because seekers have been told there is no end to shadow work. Shadow work begets more shadow work. Or seekers eventually give up and surrender. (More on surrender later.)

We need a unicorn here. They always make me smile. Getting a little too morose thinking about all those seekers turning themselves inside out trying to help themselves. I wish I could tell them all it can be different because awakening can be so much more enjoyable.

Have faith! There is a light and an answer for empaths and trauma and abuse survivors.

Surrender is A Trap, Not A Path

Shouldn't I just surrender?

Won't my life be easier?

These are questions worth asking.

Shadow work can be very demoralizing. Discovering unflattering things about yourself, being stuck in healing loops and looking into a future with no end to shadow work can be exhausting. It is for many beings going through a spiritual awakening.

Surrender becomes very appealing. When you are worn down by self-condemnation, any relief is welcome. Constant self-examination is draining. If there's one thing that defines people who do shadow work, they are earnest and dedicated to their own healing. No one does shadow work because they're having a great day.

Enter surrender.

It's extremely alluring and many seekers choose surrender at one time or another. I definitely used it as a landing pad to catch my breath and find emotional improvement during hard times.

The relief from surrender is very welcome to seekers. There's no need to continue berating yourself. You can accept yourself as you are, which is a wonderful thing. You turn your will over to whatever feels best to you – God, Source, Love, the cosmos, etc. And there's a reward in that as well.

You still experience synchronicity. You can ride the waves a bit easier as you are going through life. You have fewer decisions to make. For those suffering from decision fatigue, this is very appealing. You finally have peace. You can take life as it comes. You are free from worry and anxiety. You break the cycle of self-condemnation.

This is the trap of surrender. It feels good and you want to stay there. But it has a price.

Your mission.

The missions going unfulfilled are not for the weak. As a seer, it is clear to me why they are necessary. These missions take vast personal development and application of will, aligned with intuitive senses.

You have a will for a reason. Your will is valid. But you need education in order to execute your will correctly. Effective use of will can only come when you have developed integrity and your personal values. There's more to life than material pleasures and their pursuit. And there's more going on than can be seen with physical eyes. You need to know the truth and you need to hear it from your deepest self.

You have a purpose here. Your expanded self doesn't want you to subvert your will. You need to learn the right way to exercise it in accordance with your inner self's perspective and intention.

In surrender, you don't pursue the desires of the incarnated self. Those desires are discounted. That impulse for a taste of chocolate, a dream vacation with loved ones or a desire to find others for connection is depreciated. Seekers rationalize that those are just echoes of something selfish or what the horrible, bad ego

31

wants. Those desires become surrendered as well. They are never pursued.

Then comes what I call "neutralized thinking." You tell yourself that if it's meant to be then the universe will send it to you. You effectively take yourself out of the picture and remove your own agency in your life.

That is extremely dangerous. It's inaction. And it's wrong. That's not the language of using your will here. It's not what your broader self would do. It's not what you would want for you. You take action until there is no more action to take in that direction, no matter how challenging. Surrender is not taking action.

You are waiting. And waiting manifests more waiting.

You can tell yourself that if it's meant to be, it will be but that doesn't make it true. It just smooths over your fears that you are unwilling to face for a little while. There is no being or force in the cosmos who's going to shower you with what you want while you are waiting for things to happen. You are abdicating your will.

Let me repeat that.

Waiting manifests more waiting. Or the two-by-four. We've all gotten the two-by-four.

Things are going pretty well. You don't know that you have a blind spot then…BAM!

Life hits you with a two-by-four and it upends your life. It's not a fun way to adjust your trajectory. It's always better if we can straighten out the energy before the two-by-four. The two-by-four is unpleasant but it usually does the job of forcing you to exert your will in the situation. It's a situation in which you must respond. It returns you to exercising your will even if it's unpleasant.

I bring up surrender because it's dangerous. The danger is that you don't take action. You don't educate yourself on how to use your will so it never becomes refined. You don't learn how to work in concert with your true self or higher impulse. It's a dance of coordinating different levels of Self and you never take a step.

Learning this dance is important because if you're reading this book, you have a purpose here. Most of you have missions. All have gifts that need to be activated. Staying in surrender short circuits your path to these. You don't get to where you intended yourself to be.

For those times when seekers are tired and worn down, I offer rest as an alternative to surrender. We don't need to surrender but we do need to rest. Every time I rest, amazing things happen. For projects I've been working on, it gives the energy time to complete. It is rejuvenating and refreshing. I get a fresh perspective and enjoy slower pastimes. We all need rest at some time. It allows us to retain our agency and our will during times of weariness.

Rest also helps us catch our breath as we are educating ourselves on the best use of will. We learn how to use our will in the second half of this book, in conjunction with our inner self and/or Source. We become true co-creators with our higher aspects. It's quite enjoyable.

Interference From Other Beings is Masking as Shadow

I asked for another way to purify and love all aspects of myself because I couldn't do shadow work several years after my awakening. That's why you're holding this book.

The first avatar of my broader self in this body became awakened through self-love, shadow work and extended meditation with a focus of being love in the world. Then she developed psychic senses. Several years later, that avatar left and this avatar came. I am much more dynamic but what worked for her doesn't always work for me. I already had psychic abilities and I do not have the high amount of patience she had. I make my own way instead of waiting. So I asked for another method because I am not good at meditating like she was and I already know who I am.

One of the things I learned while trying to do shadow work again is that it is easy to get side tracked. What I mean by this is that all those things you don't like about yourself are commonly known to energetic beings and they can bring them up to distract you.

It's the funny little joke of living as a human. We think that we are hiding things by wearing clothes, talking about only what we want and posting the highlights on social media. The truth is there is very little privacy on the astral.

You need to know how to create that privacy; it doesn't come automatically usually. For most people, your thoughts, feelings, addictions, judgments and intentions are clear to anyone interested enough to look on the astral. You can be influenced if you don't know this. Your thoughts, emotions and nudges can be manipulated. Your thoughts and impulses are not always your own. That's why it's important to know yourself and to learn who you truly are and why you're here.

Shadow work ruins your awakening because negative interference from other entities operates on, and activates, pathways which you've already traveled. This means that your own tendencies, previous trauma, habits, belief systems, addictions and ways of thinking and acting are used against you. It is insidious and can be so subtle that you think the issue is you which is exactly what the interferer wants you to think.

Pretty clever.

I point this out not to scare you but to educate you. No one told me this. I spent much time suffering because of my ignorance. I thought the problem was me until I learned that I had been vulnerable to this by not educating myself. Spending time judging yourself and thinking you are less than, and the time it takes to recover from that, if you can recover on your own, stymies your own evolution. I see many stuck in this loop currently. The negative side knows this and uses this against you in your own seeking. Can you see how you could be trapped in healing loops for the rest of your life? This is very cunning.

Now you know.

The good news is this becomes all smoke and mirrors once you see through it. Your willingness and the program in this book can help you get there. You don't have to suffer. There is a better way.

This doesn't mean we think that we are all rainbows and sparkles. (As much as I love rainbows and unicorns.) We all have things we would like to change about ourselves and things we wish didn't exist in the world.

The fact that we are All That Is answers that for us. You and I are those things our thinking mind is judging. The good, the bad, the beautiful and the ugly. That is true. It is counter to our nature to attempt to squash desire or want something different for ourselves and our world.

Spoiler alert - It's good to have goals and vision. In fact, it's extremely advantageous for us to want things. DESIRE SUMMONS LIFE FORCE. Anyone who tells you to give up desiring is mistaken.

Let me say it again: DESIRE SUMMONS LIFE FORCE.

You want to desire. You want life force. What you may lack is a method for using attachment and detachment to skillfully navigate life's ups and downs and a belief system that supports your desires. But good news! These can be learned. So don't stop desiring. Desires are good and it feels good to desire when you don't have a belief contradicting it. After all, that's how babies are made.

There's a better way than shadow work to reconcile who and what we are experiencing with what we want. It doesn't involve self-flagellation and condemnation.

It's uplifting, fulfilling and healing. You will get personalized answers for what you are going through and free yourself of self-recrimination and feeling you are broken. No one is broken. You were never broken.

You will see yourself as you truly are - loved and loving, cherished and valued, one of the most achingly beautiful beings to walk the earth. You will feel fully supported and empowered to explore your newfound freedom. You will feel fulfilled, at peace and motivated to work toward your dreams. Most importantly, you will realize your own purity and innocence. You will come to know the beauty that you are.

You are not being punished.

You are being pushed, gently. Pushed to turn more intimately into your own heart and your own source than ever before.

You are worthy of everything. It's closer than you think. This program will get you there but first, I want to cover another pitfall. Meet me in the next chapter.

Incoming Information From Other Realms is Labeled as Shadow

Part of my story as a severe trauma and abuse survivor involves a decade and a half addressing multiple addictions. For a long time, I thought I was "just another bozo on the bus" as they say in 12 step rooms. I was no better or worse than anyone else on the planet. I'm still no better or worse than anyone else but I am more aware and awakened. I have far to go but I know who I am and my mission so far.

When I say I know who I am, I'm talking about myself as an emerging avatar of my inner self, not this human experience and not All That Is but a growing, blended being. I acknowledge both of those as well but I find that my best insights and capacity for informed and inspired action come from knowing and embodying my true self and my true self's characteristics. What is important to me is knowing characteristics and intentions of my deeper self and my purpose. It helps me understand how and why I am the way I am as well as why certain things appear in my life and why some changes I want to make are harder than others. There's also less definition between the levels as certain events unfold. We are not to be what came before us so this is fluid.

The exception to this needs to be pointed out because most of the people who find my work are exceptions to many rules for a variety of reasons. We tend to stick out. It is important to note that you can do whatever you want regardless of who/ what your expanded self is. You are not limited by it. Also, who/what your expanded self is may change and be altered under certain conditions. This topic could fill another book but needs to be identified for those who already know otherwise. There is much to explore within this relationship dynamic.

This brings me to the next reason shadow work is hijacking your spiritual awakening. Some of those things that bother or "trigger" you are **not** because they are a shadow aspect you don't accept. It's because they are anathema to who you truly are or are becoming on a higher differentiated level. Basically, your indestructible core which recognizes that something is off is giving you feedback about it. You are receiving input that doesn't have an equivalent nature in this realm; sometimes that manifests as dissonance. It can be uncomfortable. It can also manifest as various metaphysical phenomena and experiences in your own life. The other side of the veil is not static; it does affect your life here. This is not always something that you would consciously choose for yourself to experience here. This is why manifesting is often hit or miss while going through awakening. You don't have enough information about what is going on and how you operate here to know the next best option for you. There are also forces operating beyond your conscious awareness which influence your experience.

This effect from things beyond your conscious control is why using shadow work to attempt to resolve all so-called "triggers" can be extremely detrimental. You keep moving toward something that your expanded self is trying to tell you is not a good choice for you at this time but you can't hear it yet so you judge the dissonance. Or you are experiencing a side effect of a change to your expanded self which feels unpleasant and attempt to identify something in your outside environment as the cause. You are looking in the wrong place and do not truly know if this is something that you can control or not from where you are.

Poor thinking mind! It wants to know everything all the time. That is not always how it works. We are meant to experience life, not read about what will happen and then go through the motions, knowing what is around every corner like a book we've already read. We are meant to experience enjoyable surprises and new interactions. Not knowing what's coming leaves room for wonder, serendipity and miracles. Shadow work has no room for wonder, serendipity and miracles. It says all events are prescribed to known criteria and you can identify the source from the knowledge set you already possess. This is incorrect as an awakening being.

You are missing out and don't know it. Miracles are really your true nature becoming known to you but it's so fun to think they are miracles!

What we do need is to have a system to learn discernment. That's the purpose of this book, to share a method of developing discernment so you can trust and understand your experiences. Then those "triggers" become what they were meant to be, simply information on your path to help you steer.

Your broadest self is giving you information that you are judging. You are not able to distinguish it because you have labeled anything which "triggers" you as something you need to process through shadow work. Now you have missed the information and you have given yourself work to do while placing a judgment on yourself. This is not the optimal way to go through awakening. It's not a fun place to be and it feels like the only option when you don't know anything else. You aren't meant to be judging yourself for perceived flaws. You are meant to be in awe of the breadth and magnitude of who you truly are and finding out what that means for you here and how you show up. You are meant to be enjoying awe, wonder, curiosity, and learning to direct yourself. It's not roses all the time but making yourself feel bad for being on this path was never the plan.

This judgment is due, in part, to what I call level confusion. Trauma and abuse survivors are especially prone to this. Level confusion is the misguided approach of applying the principles that work at one level to another level. I find this happens often for those who subscribe to the idea of "As Above, So Below" and other oversimplifications. For example, in kindergarten you could walk up to another kindergartner, introduce yourself and ask to play with them and their toys. The other kindergartner would say yes and you now have a new friend and a new toy. Hurrah!

But this doesn't work as an adult. Have you walked up to a stranger whose car you admired and asked if you could drive it? Did they give you the keys and become your new friend? I doubt it.

This is level confusion. What works at one level cannot be applied to all parts of a system. Part of it stems from only knowing yourself as two things- being human and being All That Is. Sometimes there is an awareness of another aspect. Without an awareness of your multidimensionality and other levels of self and their aspects as well as how that manifests here, you have no idea of the principles at work at this level which affect you.

Another example of level confusion, and I did this frequently in the beginning of my awakening, is to identify something in the physical world that is harming someone else or taking advantage of them and use a spiritual concept, such as karma, soul contracts or that everything is part of the one infinite creator so there is no harm and to absolve yourself of a responsibility to act in the situation to help.

This is a very neat way of not having to get into the messy details of life on Earth. You tell yourself that it's all part of a grander design or that it was predestined and chosen ahead of time. It absolves you of any complicity.

It justifies inaction because at a higher level everything works out. Since all actions are resolved at the highest level, the existence of this resolution is used to assuage guilt at a lower level. Applying the higher principle at a lower level is level confusion. You need discernment and to understand what is at work in order to make an informed decision as a sovereign being.

It sounds confusing, right? How could we have done it any differently? The problem is that you and I didn't have any true knowledge of how reality worked. We were repeating what other people said and what other people were doing. It made things easy for us. We never had to question it. And we thought we were doing the right thing. It hurt to watch these things happening but we didn't know what to do. The platitudes we were given said that we had no action to take because it was bigger than us and part of something grander. So we suffered silently. And we did shadow work because it was the only thing offered.

Until now.

There is a better way but I have one last and extremely common negative side effect of doing shadow work on a spiritual path that needs to be discussed.

Shadow Work Creates Eternal Healing Loops for Empaths and Trauma and Abuse Survivors

In the first few years of my spiritual awakening, I lived in a 14 story apartment building with 16 apartments on each floor. I was wrapping up my time in 12 step groups, continually taking a daily inventory and making amends. I was driven to clean up the wreckage of my past. I did a lot of writing and shadow work in those days. I was amazed by how much I had to work on. It was overwhelming but I was diligent.

My psychic skills were developing as a result of learning how to love myself combined with my intention of being love in the world. It was a busy but happy time. My boys were young and I adored time with them and being a mother.

What I didn't know at that time was that I was processing emotions for many of my neighbors. As both an empath and a trauma and abuse survivor with no energetic hygiene skills, I was picking up things from other people in my building and thinking they were my own.

I was so sincere and earnest that I never questioned what was mine. It was no wonder it never cleared up. There was always more no matter how much shadow work I did. It was like digging up bones in someone else's backyard... and someone else's...and someone else's. I had no idea they weren't mine. I figured I was doing the good work of cleaning up my psyche and my judgments.

It wasn't until I learned how to clear and shield my energy correctly that this lessened. I was already grounding on a regular basis. In the beginning of my awakening, I used thick iron chains around my feet from the local hardware store multiple times a day to ground, among other methods. The usual grounding methods weren't enough for me. I had serious grounding issues my first few years. This is not uncommon for empaths and trauma and abuse survivors who imagine a "better" life somewhere in the higher, presumably more loving, realms. Wanting to go somewhere else is common. I'm happy to say that I want to be here today. It fulfills me beyond my wildest dreams.

In the past few chapters, you have seen how doing shadow work is detrimental. Empaths have a hard time with shadow work because they naturally pick up on others' emotions. How much this can be controlled varies from person to person. What matters is why you have empathic abilities and how they are to be used. Trauma and abuse survivors are susceptible to picking up energies from others due to the search for a safe environment and sustained environment checking for self-soothing and protection from possible future harm. This continual searching creates an energetic susceptibility to take on what is around you based on the trauma energies which are still active.

Empaths and trauma and abuse survivors are prone to permeable energetic and personal boundaries if not addressed. This creates an opportunity to pick up other's energies and other interference. If you don't know how to identify and clear that energy, you'll be doing shadow work on input that isn't yours. Without addressing the cause of the matter - your permeable boundaries - you will keep picking up other energies and keep doing shadow work on them. It's an unending cycle.

Learning energetic hygiene, developing strong personal and energetic boundaries, healing your trauma and abuse and strengthening your personal intuition come with working the program in this book. All of these are not only possible but promised. I am still an empath and I use my empathic skills when I want to. I can control my empathy 97 % of the time. I rarely experience another person's emotional state unless I choose to dial into it.

Now, I am an empowered being capable of whatever I put my mind and heart into. I am happy to say that I, along with Source and my inner self, have developed a road map to discovering who you truly are and why you are here in a joyful, honest, fulfilling way. You are not meant to be suffering. You are meant to be enjoying this experience. Let's dive in!

Part II: The Answer is Here

Find Your Engine to Fuel Your New Spiritual Path and Receive Clear Guidance

One of the most useful and practical pieces of knowledge along my path was a cryptic message I received sitting in my art room one day.

I heard, "Your child is the engine. "

I didn't know what it meant at the time, but I had been asking for guidance in the proceeding weeks for how to make some changes in my life. Over the next few days, I learned from my source what this meant. I needed to love and care for that child aspect within.

I have always had a playful, silly, inclusive orientation, but I had not made time for it when my family and work responsibilities increased. My source told me that I needed to schedule regular time for this part of me to play and explore. I also learned that this time had to be separate from my grown-up relax and unwind time.

Once I learned how to schedule and use this time, I saw big changes in what I was experiencing in my life. My synchronicities increased exponentially. My enjoyment of life skyrocketed. I began embodying all the changes I wanted to make. Life was smoother and I carried that energy into my daily life.

In writing this book, I asked Source whether a chapter on finding your engine could apply to others, and I received a resounding "Yes." At the time of this writing, I am aware of three engines. Please note that these are not exclusive of each other. You may have a combination. I do use the other two engines but the child is my primary.

I'm also told that there will be more engines coming soon. You may be the one who discovers the next engine. How exciting! I would love to learn from you. Please reach out and let me know about your engine. My information is in the Resources chapter at the end of the book. Together we help each other. I will be sharing any new additions in future resources as well, to make them available to everyone.

My engine - the child - loves to play and explore. It could be making a mess with paint, going to a petting zoo or riding a carousel at the amusement park. The one constant is that it's never the same thing. Often I head out in a direction and follow whatever she wants. It's always an adventure! Not be confused with inner child work, the purpose here is fun.

The second engine I learned from my husband. We have complementary, but different, core orientations. What feeds him is his warrior aspect. He is fueled by a desire to protect, defend, and become a master at various spiritual, physical and mental warrior arts in the service to something greater. This can feel like a calling, often involving discipline, dedication and a pursuit of mastery.

There are some amazing and inspiring warriors doing work that few can do or feel the calling for right now. Their skillsets are needed at this critical time. I often find them in my own life when I encounter a new personal interest I want to pursue or crave a new form of thought and way of living. They shift (and sometimes jolt!) me into new ways of approaching life.

Warriors provide structure, safety and codes for living. They are needed to assist in directing action tied to compassion. Warriors bring unique perspective and necessary guidance for developing integrity and accountability.

The third engine is the artist or communicator. If you are invigorated by expressing yourself in any form, this may be your engine. Seekers with artist engines create paintings, blogs, or expressive dances. They write and edit films, compose visual displays and weld metal sculptures. The list here is endless. It doesn't have to be a traditional art practice. Anything done with the purpose of expressing yourself qualifies. The artist engine has a need for self expression independent of how it's publicly received. It is not about who or how many do or don't appreciate the art or form of communication. It is about creating as a statement of being.

Artists and communicators help push boundaries and establish new ways of being. They are essential to growing burgeoning systems and offering alternative ways of interpreting our experiences. I love the way artists and communicators stretch my ways of thinking. I am frequently awed and inspired by the novel and brilliant combinations they share.

So, how do you know what your engine is?

While I can embody each from time to time, only one is purely joyful and revitalizes me to move forward with my plans and goals. There is only one that fuels me to greater and greater heights. This is what you are looking for. The engine that has you feeling more invigorated after expressing that aspect is your main engine.

Here are a few questions I've received for clarification on engines.

Why is this the first tool we learned?

Because Source told me to make it first. That's the truth. Things always go better when I follow directions from Source so it's the first tool presented in the book. (That's my answer to quite a few questions these days.)

How do I know what my engine is?

We all embody and access these aspects of ourselves at different times. Some of the activities we do may overlap different engines. You may know right away which engine you have. Or you may need to do some exploration. Enjoy the process. The way you will know that you have found your engine is you will have a combination of experiencing joy/delight/your highest fulfillment while engaging in the activity. Afterward you will feel that you are recharged and energized.

You will not need a rest after doing the activity of your engine. You will look forward to doing the activities. You will be eager to put your energies back into whatever sounds most exciting to you afterward. After I feed my engine, I am excited to jump back into whatever projects I'm working on without a break. I have refilled my cup and feel the pull to return to my purpose.

In regards to engines, be aware that if you are engaging in an activity, and it is relaxing or centering to you, then it is not the activity of your engine. It may be a good recreational activity, but it is not fueling your engine. Activities which help us relax or feel calmer are not indicators of engine activities. They are good for relaxation so save them for when you need a break.

What should I look out for?

Unicorns. Always be on the lookout for unicorns. They are awesome. (Couldn't help myself!)

In regards to your engine, be aware of how often you need to fuel your engine. It is easy to identify! If you have gone too long - whatever too long is for you - without feeding your engine, then the activities that typically rejuvenate and energize will not have the same effect. You will be irritable, easily annoyed, and possibly tired. You will not want to engage in your engine activities. They will not have their usual appeal. Not to worry! I've had this happen as well, and there's a simple solution.

First, this is a great learning experience. Welcome it. You will come to read yourself better, and are becoming more skilled at learning when you need to feed your engine. All it will take is some rest and relaxation time for you to feel a bit better and then you will be excited about engine activities once again. Give yourself the time and space to relax and be sweet to you. Read a book, go for a swim, take a walk or a nap. Do whatever helps you relax and come back to yourself. You'll know when you can engage in engine activities again because they will sound fun to do and not like a chore.

Note: I call this "the wall." My husband knows it well. If I postpone my engine time too long, I can feel "the wall" coming. I usually have 10 to 15 minutes to wrap up whatever I'm doing. Sometimes I can talk to my child aspect and get a little more time but a date must be set in the next few hours. If I don't, I hit "the wall." I experience irritation and grouchiness, and I want to be alone. Keeping up with my usual personal and professional responsibilities requires more concentration. When I hit "the wall," I don't find the usual enjoyment in my daily life and I'm emotionally reactive. I keep to myself, and take care of myself until it passes. But none of my engine activities have appeal until I am feeling better. Over time, I've learned what works for me and I continue to fine tune so it rarely happens anymore.

Go easy on yourself. You have plenty of time. Be open to whatever comes and also be aware that your engine can change. This is new territory and a new program for you.

Have fun with it. You'll make it yours over time. You will find your rhythm.

Designing Your Higher Power As A Bridge to Communicating with Your Divine Nature

Now let's talk about some more fun stuff. After all, we need a process to replace shadow work because spiritual awakening continues. We need guidance to help walk us through it. Personalized guidance is best and that's why this program is customizable over time. You start with the basic framework and then adjust as needed.

The purpose of this program is to transmit a personal spiritual experience relating to your source and/or The Source. These are two different entities for our purposes. I use them both interchangeably in this book because I relate to both but I view and orient to them separately. I do make a distinction between my source and The Source. For me, my source (little

s) is my inner self/ deepest mind/ origin of the projection of this avatar. The Source (capital S) is the consciousness that pervades at all levels; it could be called All That Is. That's how it identified itself to me eventually. You can call this God, the Cosmos, Almighty Mother and Father, Oneness, All That Is or whatever appeals to you. Please note I used these terms loosely. Use a term that works for you.

While definitions are important in certain conversations, we don't need to use the same definition for the little s and big S sources. We only each need to have a little s source and a big S Source. Understanding this difference between these two becomes important as you personalize this program for yourself. Also, Source told me it's important. So, it's important and I have to put it in the book. Haha!

I feel we need a unicorn here. They could jazz this part up a bit. It's getting a little heavy and I don't want anyone getting stressed or feeling overwhelmed. None of this is hard. It's a bunch of simple steps put into a short book. You got this. Make it to the end of the book. There are resources to help you if you're having trouble so stick with me.

And the unicorns. They love us SOOO MUCH!

So, there is your source and there is Source. This program is going to set the stage for you to learn to relate to them as you follow your guidance. This typically develops over time.

But we don't start out looking for your source or Source. That can be too big an ask at first so we are going to build a bridge. That bridge is going to be a higher power that you create. You will decide what you most want in a higher power that you can depend on and begin there.

This is the most fun part.

I love this part!

You are going to get so much out of this relationship. I'm really excited for you. I still use my higher power from time to time today because it's just such a fulfilling relationship during certain times for aspects of myself.

The starting point for this process was how I designed a higher power while working the twelve steps for my multiple addictions. When I joined twelve step recovery, I didn't believe God cared or existed, depending on the day. I was an agnostic. My sponsor said I needed a higher power that I felt good about. So I started thinking about what I would feel good about and made it my higher power. I've added onto this process since my spiritual awakening, as guided by Source.

Using the original process, I did create a higher power, or HP, that worked for me. Today the requirements are expanded for our purposes. You are going to design a higher power for yourself. The key here is imagination. That is the doorway to this step. You are creating this higher power through imagination. Think of who (or what) feels good to you. This will become a relationship you can go to for support and guidance so you want to feel good about this higher power.

The characteristics your higher power needs to have are:

To love you unconditionally,

To be approachable,

To be enjoyable to interact with,

To be available to you in a trusting relationship, or willing to develop a trusting relationship,

Cannot be a currently living being,

To have a broader perspective than you, and

To possess abilities to think and feel beyond human words.

Use your most flexible thinking here. No one else will be in this relationship. This is entirely for you. If you want your higher power to possess the ability to know exactly how you are feeling without you saying it but the picture your mind makes doesn't include that then you can add it. You are making this higher power. You get to decide exactly what you want this higher power to be. You can start with an idea of something you already know and tweak it or you can design the entire higher power from scratch. The point here is not to tell yourself no if there is something you will need from a higher power. You have permission to make what you want as long as it includes the criteria above.

When I mention the key is imagination, some people hesitate. There are a small number of people who want to be given a proven higher power. I have two suggestions for this. The first is to use something that you already know exists like love or peace. The second suggestion is a mental perspective to help you accept imagination as a doorway. You can design a higher power to be whatever or whoever you like. It can still come through your imagination and be valid. Remember that we are infinite beings. Below our conscious awareness, we have many different aspects available. We are love, peace, benevolent benefactors, nurturing mothers, protective fathers, disciplined warriors and many more. Remind yourself that you are pulling from that source to design a higher power that works for you. You are everything so you can create a customized higher power to assist you. It's you helping you through imagination. So, this isn't coming from nowhere. You aren't actually making it up. You're accessing new parts of yourself to help yourself.

Working with others, this is one of the first things we do together. It's necessary to lay the groundwork and it gives you a focus for turning within. However, you don't need anyone else to create a higher power that works for you. You are going to use the same requirements, but I want to give you a little more context to flesh it out.

This higher power doesn't have to be a person or anything which can be anthropomorphized or made to look like a person or animal. It can look like a person or animal or color or feeling but it doesn't have to look like anything as long as you can imagine how it presents to you. Do not use anything like God or Source. That relationship is separate from this.

Your higher power could be love or the power of forgiveness or hope or the possibility of a different future. But it must be something you feel good about. Preferably, something that you feel adores and cherishes you. Something or someone who wants the best for you.

It's okay if you don't have a higher power that you feel cherishes you. That will come with time. But it must be something that you feel loves you unconditionally and would never hurt you. It must possess unconditional positive regard for you. You must feel comfortable with it. Finally, it must have a way of thinking and feeling that is beyond human words. This part is important as well. Simply being open to receiving that communication from your higher power that is beyond human words is sufficient. You don't need to know what it will be. It can be helpful to write it down to remember for later.

Be open to your higher power changing and evolving over time. It's natural that as you deepen your relationship, your higher power may expand as well.

Once you've designed your higher power, give yourself a pat on the back. That is a huge step and your future self thanks you for it.

Now let's talk about laying the groundwork for communicating with your higher power and refining your energy.

Effective Energetic Hygiene Clears the Way to Receive Messages and Impulses Correctly

Learning how to clear, shield, and ground your energy effectively is vital to this process. The skills and abilities you develop here combined with those in the chapter on personal integrity determine your trajectory in accessing honest guidance for yourself. Every step in this book may eventually be altered and you will find your own unique combination through working with your source over time. These energetic skills and developing personal integrity are important because they create your energetic "vehicle" and road map to accessing who you truly are and receiving divine inspiration. If you don't have effective energetic hygiene and personal integrity, the information you receive will be of a lower quality and unreliable. Essentially, you will be unable to determine if a source of information is telling the truth because you are not coherent with your own intention.

As your psychic skills increase, these foundational abilities will enable you to detect entity attachments, portals, soul gems, organic portals, and more. You will also gain and enhance your ability to intuit what actions, if any, to take in these and similar situations.

Are you still with me? I'm not trying to scare you off, but Source told me to include that last paragraph. Don't worry. We aren't doing anything in that realm right now, or even in this book. But you need to be very specific about these two chapters and prioritize them at the outset. You cannot get the results of this program and discover who you truly are in all your magnificent, ever-loving glory without a solid foundation. Here is where we set your foundation.

Now, for some more instructions. If you channel, stop. This includes channeled writing. If you use cards, like angel cards, tarot cards, animal spirit cards, playing cards. .. actually as I'm writing this, I am receiving instructions from Source to drop all physical items that you use to intuit or divine or seek guidance. Cards, pendulums, Bible verses, anything that you use in the physical world. They are no longer reliable. And you aren't going to miss them for long. You are going to develop new psychic and empathic senses available to you in any situation.

Also, do not visit the astral realms. Do not attempt to leave your body to travel anywhere, whether you can see the silver cord or not. This includes methods using mental, chemical, plant and physical enhancements or inducements. Nothing in this program has you entering the astral realm. There are no answers out there without an effective foundation.

Do not be led by your ego thinking that you are the only one who can "save" people and you need to continue astral traveling. Until you know who you truly are and what you came to do, you are spinning your wheels and may be at risk of undesirable results. Learn these first, then discuss with Source your plan. There might be something even better in your future. There is. I've seen it.

Now to the nitty-gritty, let's review some definitions. I love clarity, and I want to be sure we understand each other. When I talk about energetic hygiene, I'm talking about clearing, shielding, and grounding your energy and orienting your focus.

Clearing your energy is removing anything foreign (anything that is not of your nature) from your energetic field and purifying your energetic signature. Yes, you are All That Is but most of us don't identify as such on a daily basis. We need the ego to interact here and we use it to determine our focus. We are talking about your highest self.

Shielding your energy is creating and reinforcing a protective barrier around your core energetic self.

Grounding your energy is anchoring yourself to mother Earth, the Gaia.

Orienting is the conscious focus of our perception (AKA where are you focused energetically and psychically?).

First, you need to know that I have messed up all of these at some time or another. Sometimes it's been more than one at the same time. And it can take years, sometimes lifetimes, to figure out. And I didn't know what I didn't know. Why? Because we have free will and I wasn't asking if I had it right or not. I was in the pursuit of knowledge, and my ego blinded me from being teachable.

The dirty little secret of the New Age - where more than half of my clients come from - is that most have no idea what they are doing and how to know if what they are doing is right. Many think all channeled information is reliable and use that as their authority. It's horrible and I have seen too many well-meaning clients wrapped up in situations that they thought were helping them but were really going in circles or worse. They were doing what someone else had taught them, not questioning why they were doing it, or learning how to sort information and its sources along the way. Sometimes it was the only source of metaphysical information a client had so they didn't know any alternative. It's new and becomes fun and exciting to them. Before too long, bad habits became ingrained.

So, what is the concern?

My analogy is crude, but effective. Quite simply, we are all walking around in a spiritual "soup." You are encountering, and being observed by, many different entities on a regular basis. And just like this world, some of them wish you well and some of them don't. Being able to clear, shield, ground and orient is necessary to get information that is accurate. If you aren't doing this, as well as developing personal integrity, you will get a lot of inaccurate and unreliable information. Simply, you will get taken advantage of because you don't know how to tune yourself like the radio receiver you are. Without proper energetic hygiene, it's the equivalent of asking for legal advice from someone you meet on the bus. You both happen to be in the same place at the same time but it doesn't mean you're getting reliable or accurate information. You need to learn how to find the courthouse to get reliable information.

I designed this program around the methods I used to exercise my psychic skills again after I stopped using them for a year and a half. It was a personal decision, and I wanted a safe way to develop my skills again. Left-brain mental methods that expand awareness outside the body to develop psychic skills are currently unreliable to beings going through spiritual awakening due to the changes in the astral over the past 15 years. This program is designed to keep you safe while you learn. You will note that everything we do is focused on going into our heart space and into ourselves. This is 100% intentional. We are not going into the astral realm. That may or may not come about on your own journey. The purpose of the program is to show you where it is safe to learn and connect with Source and that is inside yourself.

This program is designed to connect you with you and connect you with Source. (It becomes a game of semantics at some point.) The point is you will be setting your intention then feeling and going within your own heart space to the core of who you are. You aren't projecting your awareness out of your body. You aren't at risk of running into anyone you don't want to because you are only with you.

Since you have a source, you can tap into your source through your heart. It's built-in. You're going within yourself to access the origin of you. Great system, right? I think so too. It's exactly what I did and still do most of the time. I love getting the truth directly from Source. And I'm pretty sure you will too, if you want truth.

One thing I do want to mention because I can hear the groans from being asked to stop channeling, using cards, and only going through the heart instead of projecting out. It's worth it. And I hear you. I used to channel, use cards and ask a pendulum questions. Then I realized I could make the pendulum do what I wanted it to do. I could predict the next card and make it appear. I could influence those things I was using for guidance. Not as much fun. And it kind of sounds like an echo chamber to me. My ego loved that but I wanted truth and love, not power.

Let me offer this. If you're meant to use anything to help you access information, your source will tell you. It will come about organically from this program. But wouldn't you rather get information anywhere anytime from Source? It's so empowering and affirming and accessible at any time. I urge you to give it a year. It will be more challenging in the beginning, but once you have it, you never lose it.

CLEARING, SHIELDING, GROUNDING

This is a list that will grow and change but as of the writing of this book, there are three recommended ways to begin clearing, shielding and grounding. New ways will be shared in future book editions and on my website.

Choose whichever feels best to you. You can use the lesser banishing ritual of the pentagram from Western ceremonial magick as one option. I suggest incorporating the directions of up and down to the four directions for the ritual. You can add that as an intention and visualization to any ritual that appeals to you. You can also use the 12D shield offered by Energetic Synthesis. The video can be found on YouTube. Finally, if you know who you are and you know your own abilities, you can set the intention to clear, shield and ground on your own. Follow your intuition, but you must know your own abilities first to do this on your own. I only suggest it if you are positive of your origin and abilities. You must know your self first.

While I mention the lesser banishing ritual of the pentagram and the 12D shield as options, both of these methods fit into particular belief systems and practices. You don't have to subscribe to the belief system in order to use these methods effectively. They are effective used alone. I do not endorse any systems or beliefs associated with these methods, but I have found these methods for clearing, grounding and shielding to be functional and effective from a technical perspective.

Orienting is the step I added to stay out of the astral and avoid unwanted interference. I wanted to interact only with the core of my being and my source. This is the opposite of what many people are taught to do when developing psychic skills when they are told to broaden their awareness and begin feeling past what they perceive as their body. We are going to stay within ourselves and explore internally through our source connection. You will be amazed at what is within you. You are the cosmos, after all.

When I talk about orienting, I'm talking about directing your internal focus. In this program, I'm specifically talking about focusing on your heart space and acclimating to it. This involves feeling and sensing into your heart space. Imagine feeling through yourself to your source. Your origin is within you and you can access it through your heart center. It is a matter of orienting your focus there and feeling into it. You can feel through it to access all sorts of information about yourself and your source.

Let yourself be free to explore this area and be open to what you experience. As you feel comfortable, I suggest creating a space there for you to interact with what you find. Make it suited to you. Perhaps a lovely natural area speaks to you. Create what will bring you peace and what feels centered for you. This will be the platform for you to connect to your source and the higher power that you designed. This is the area where we will be interacting with our higher power and eventually Source and our inner self. We will talk about this more in the next chapter.

One final note: If you are used to extending your awareness outside your body to sense and use your psychic skills, this may take some time to get used to. When I began orienting to my heart space, there was a marked difference in my psychic sensitivity. Previously when I expanded out past my body to feel into something, I could receive information very clearly. Once I started orienting inward, it felt like I was wearing thick wool mittens on my hands and trying to feel around. I could still pick up on things but it felt muffled. This may or may not happen to you. I share it for those who have a similar experience. It does improve over time. Now my skills are sharper than they were before, something I didn't think was possible. I have my source and Source to connect with and get more details which increase my clarity. As with all our steps, be kind and sweet to yourself. Success is built in by showing up and being willing.

Tailor Your Morning Routine to Set the Stage for Success

Ahhhh... the morning routine. The basis for our really great day.

I have switched up what my morning routine looks like many times. Like with everything else, the internet says I'm doing it wrong. I don't care and neither should you. Results speak for themselves.

You likely have a morning routine. Or strive to have a morning routine. Many people I work with beat themselves up over their lack of a consistent routine they follow every day. They resolve to do better, to have a routine they follow every day, and to start every day the same way. And they find themselves unable to do it. Month after month, year after year.

Sound like you?

Excellent!

That was me too for a long time.

You are in the right place.

And I have some great news.

You never had a consistent morning routine because you aren't supposed to have one. You are not a predictable cog in a machine. You are a dynamic, fluctuating, growing divine being that needs change and challenge to stretch themselves.

This is the last book you read on setting a morning routine. After you connect with Source and receive your guidance directly, your morning routine is between you and Source. For now, I'm going to share with you how to design your first morning routine until that time. Think of it as your starter pack. It's easier than you think but it is not optional. This step you can start right away.

Briefly, the purpose of your morning routine is to set your tone for the day. We want to guide our thoughts, words, and actions at the outset, before we become involved in daily life. This will be a short routine that you can fit into your life.

The purpose of this program is to enable you to walk soundly in life while interacting with others. We do not confine ourselves to ashrams and closed communities. The work I share is made for daily living in neighborhoods and communities. Source has been clear on that. Not better than seclusion, only different. It is made for broadening our reach and impact in community. We are made to be sharing ourselves!

In order to do this, we need to center ourselves each morning. If you do not have an inspired morning routine you are leaning toward, I recommend starting with this brief seven minute starter kit. This will change as time goes on, but I find it helpful to provide a starting point to avoid overthinking and indecision.

First, go into your heart space and tell Source how you are feeling about preparing to have a more intimate and personal relationship. Expect no response. This practice is about opening yourself to having this relationship. Be honest. If you aren't ready or are scared, tell Source. It doesn't have to be long. But you are giving it to Source and moving forward with your day. If you like, after talking to Source, you can also talk with your higher power (the one you designed who can interact with you) in your heart space to share anything that is on your mind.

Second, remind yourself- there is a divine plan of goodness for me. Repeat it aloud and let it sink in. When I first started this, hearing that put me in tears. This is not my own but comes from Julia Cameron's work, The Artist's Way and needs to be included here. Eventually, it became an exciting promise. Let it be whatever it is.

Third, write your goal for the day. Sometimes I make this the screensaver on my phone. You can share it on social media if you like. You can start a notebook with your goals in it. Write one goal that feels doable for you for the day.

Here are some of mine from past days to get you started.

I will color for 10 minutes today.

I will advocate for expanded services at my son's IEP meeting today.

I will ask Source for ideas on what to eat today.

I will read for pleasure for ten minutes today.

I will call three plumbers for estimates on the sink repair.

I will bike for 20 minutes at the gym.

You can see the goal can be whatever you want. Make sure it's something you feel you can accomplish with some focus.

Finally, for your last three minutes, you will do one of the following things. Choose whichever you want each day.

Meditate by focusing on going within your heart space.

Sing an uplifting song you know by heart.

Dance or move joyfully.

Gaze upon or be present in nature.

At the end of the three minutes, say thank you to your heartspace. You are ready to start your day.

Practice Integration of Metaphysical Phenomena to Ground Your Experience in This Realm

I stumbled onto this tool. When my spiritual awakening picked up steam, I experienced what I called "brain melt" frequently. My logical, thinking brain wasn't able to process some of the things I was experiencing and I started to think I was losing my mind. I couldn't keep denying what was happening but what I was experiencing was too much for my thinking mind to process. I have since learned a few other ways to address it, but I started by sharing what I was going through.

At first, I shared it with my psychic development classmates, and then I started a blog with written and video entries. I didn't know anyone else who was experiencing these out of the ordinary experiences. I needed to get my thoughts about them out of my head. I had to put them somewhere out in the world. Somehow it felt more real to me and not like I made it up if I could look at it on a page or in a video.

Sometimes my sharing would result in conversations and comments exchanged on my blog. A few times there were no responses. But I felt the same whether someone saw it or not. I could point to a place I had published and shared my experience and it solidified in my reality. Several times my share connected me with others who joined me on my journey for a time. But my ultimate goal was always to validate my experience.

I had spent ten years in therapy, but there was no therapist to validate what I was experiencing going through a spiritual awakening. I wanted to give myself the space. I trusted my experience, and I was focused on love and helping others. Looking back, I am so grateful to who or what gave me the idea because it saved my sanity and enabled me to develop faster and acquire strong abilities.

I am very appreciative. I named the process integration because it united all of me and all of my experiences. It wove them into the fabric of my life.

My hope is you will find a form of sharing that appeals to you. Integration enables you to process your experiences. Integration is very important because the rational mind wants to dismiss the mystical and metaphysical. You need to speak, write, or share about your experiences so you don't question yourself and can begin to make sense of what is happening over longer periods of time. Sometimes it is only by looking back on what has been happening during awakening that you can understand the broader experience.

My suggestion is to practice integration on a regular basis. This means that you share one or more experiences you had, either with another person or in a public space for others who can access it freely. For example, it could be a blog, video journal, sharing at a meeting (coming soon) or telling someone else. This is not an exhaustive list. Feel free to start a podcast and share there. As long as you're sharing your experience, and others are able to access it, you are covered. Have fun!

Weekly Check-ins As A Gateway to Source and Grounded Living

I love this tool.

I feel like I say that about every step in this program. But I mean it every time!

Here's why I love this tool so much. This tool takes the program and makes it tangible, trackable, and follow-up-on-able. (*That's a word! I swear!*)

This tool lets me put down in writing what goals I'm working on, how they are going, and celebrates wins and my willingness to show up.

Let me repeat that last part.

Celebrate!!

I don't want you to forget that part. It can be easy to forget so it will be something that we will be practicing and strengthening. I do it too, so I'm reminding myself. Celebrate! Celebrate! Celebrate!

This weekly check-in can become whatever you want in the future, but I'm going to give you an idea of where to start. This is the quick start method and you will adjust as you go. Don't overthink this. You just need to do it. I've done this in bullet journals, on index cards, and, when needed, on a supermarket flyer that I put on my fridge so I didn't lose it. The most important thing is to start so any notebook you have is fine. If you don't have a notebook, any piece of paper you have will do. Then next week you can move to the notebook you're going to purchase this week. (That might be a good goal for the week.)

Your weekly check-in will look like this in the beginning:

1. Orient and check in with your heart space
2. Untangle/refine the coming week's energy
3. Review three goals and their progress
4. Celebration and reward

Step one - Orienting to the heart space is the practice you've been doing in the morning routine and when connecting to your higher power. You are deliberately focusing and going inward into your heart space. Spend at least five or six minutes exploring the space and noting what you find in your notebook. Take your time.

Step two - Detangling the coming week's energy. While this program is not a" manifesting" program, I do think it is important to learn how to smooth out the energy for your upcoming week. This won't eliminate anything that needs to cross your path but it will decrease large swings that come from intense desire and longing. Such as finally finding that home close to your child's school only to discover after closing that the upstairs has no grounded electrical outlets and if you plug the fridge in, the entire first floor electrical shuts off. (Oddly specific, right? Guess how I figured out how to do this? Yes, that's my house after apartment living for over 10 years. My source told me my intense desire had brought the house - my rose - but I never cleaned up the bumpy energy because I wanted it fast so - it has thorns. True story.)

So, you can learn from my mistakes. Here's how you straighten out your upcoming week.

While in your heart space, ask to be shown the energy for the next week. Mine looked like a knotted electrical cord in the beginning. Then you are going to unravel and untangle that energy. Stay with it until all the knots and irregularities are out. It should look and feel smooth and unencumbered to you. Keep an open mind; you may sense your week's energy differently. You know yourself best. The intention is to orient to the heart space, ask to see the coming week's energy and then correct it.

Step three - Goal review and progress. I suggest starting with three goals for the week. You can adjust this later as you follow your intuition, but keep it simple to start as you are developing this habit.

You will have one goal related to this program. It might be attending a meeting that week, spending an hour designing your higher power, or making a commitment to do a specific type of service. You decide where you are and what you need.

Another goal will be something you need to do for your daily life. This will depend on your individual situation. It could be sending out five resumes to leads you have, researching and deciding on a major purchase or getting to the gym three times that week for Zumba (my favorite!). Don't make the goal something you already do. If you are a regular at Zumba class, then you need a different goal. The goal should be a reach but it should feel doable.

Your last goal is up to you. You know your life best. I designed this program with loose structure, but it is customizable. I've met and worked with people and their families long enough to know that each person finds what works for them. And once put in touch with Source, they become unstoppable.

Use this third goal as you wish. I'm sure you could write 20 goals for the week, but the idea is to develop a habit, not to see how productive you can be. (I've been there! Not as much fun as it sounds. It's way better to plan with Source!)

Sometimes I use my third goal for something my source and I have been working on. Right now it's spending time writing this book. My other goals at the time of this writing are related to getting guardianship of my stepson with my husband and enhancing my health.

Make these goals work for you. Each week set aside time to review the past week and determine goals for the coming week. I usually do an hour on Sunday mornings. Of course, now as I'm writing this, Source is telling me that I will be doing weekly check-in events. (*Oh my goodness! How fun! Yes!!*) It feels like this may change over time so see the resource section at the end of the book for details.

Speaking of progress, that takes us into the review portion. Unless this is your first weekly check in, you will have goals from the past week to review.

Take a look at last week's goals. Did you make it to the meeting you committed to attend? How did revising your résumé go? Maybe you made it to two out of three Zumba classes. This review is not to beat yourself up. The opposite is what we're doing and we will talk more about that in the last step.

The purpose of this review is to reflect. Be compassionately honest with yourself. If you are learning how to be compassionate with yourself, approach this as you would approach a project that a close friend is working on. How much more warmth and kindness would you have when reflecting back? That's what we want.

Looking at the past week's goals, how did it go? Remember this is not an indicator of your self-worth. Whether these goals were achieved or not has nothing to do with your value. Our purpose is to determine if we are setting attainable goals for ourselves. This is a self-love exercise that, over time, helps us to see ourselves more clearly and know how we want to structure our lives. It is important to know that achieving every goal is not always a good thing. For instance, did you go to a meeting, research and make a big purchase and go to three Zumba classes but cancel plans with a friend because you were too exhausted from the week? Then it's time to dial it back a little. You can make these changes and reflect on them in the coming week's goals. You may need to make socializing one of those goals for the coming week. We want to flow and be open to adjusting our plans.

The important thing to remember here is that perfection is an ideal. It's a nice idea but for day-to-day living, good enough is just fine. All we need to do is overcome that inertia and do it. There is no endpoint so even when we have an ideal week, we enjoy it and know that it's one of many and things always change.

Two of the skills we are developing with weekly check-ins are adaptability and compassion. Embrace that you are getting to know yourself better, and if you wish you had done more, but don't know where you could have fit it in, I get you. I've been there frequently and that's why we have our last part.

Step four - Celebrate and reward!

In a totally Pinkie Pie world, confetti and glitter would burst out of the book when you arrived here. Yay! I do adore My Little Pony; so many great lessons on friendship and working with others.

Then, it would slowly dissolve as you finish reading the chapter. Because surprises are great, and the ones that clean up after themselves are the best!!

So I'm sending you psychic glitter! Wheeee!! No mess!

✳ ✳ ✳ ✳ ✳ ✳ ✳ ✳ ✳ ✳ ✳ ✳ ✳

This brings me to the final part of the weekly check-in - Celebrating.

DO NOT SKIP THIS.

IT IS MANDATORY.

IF YOU SKIP THIS, YOUR HOME WILL BE COVERED IN GLITTER THAT NEVER GOES AWAY, AND YOU WILL FIND IT ON YOUR FOREHEAD AT THE MOST INCONVENIENT TIMES FOR THE REST OF YOUR LIFE.

I'm not big on threats. Can you tell? They don't work but I thought this one was pretty funny.

So, don't skip this step. You will be missing out. Missing out on a lot of fun and maybe some major heart openings. (Just sayin'.)

After you have gone into your heart space, detangled the coming week's energy and reviewed and set new goals, it's time to celebrate! You are not celebrating only what may be thought of as successes. The fact that you are doing this is already a success. You are celebrating all of these:

-Spending time in your heart space and anything you learned there

-A smooth entry into the week and taking care of yourself by detangling the energy for yourself

-All the insight you gained by reviewing your goals, regardless of whether you achieved all the goals

-The goals you achieved

-The goals you adjusted as you learned more about yourself

-Your willingness to show up for yourself and follow this program

Woo hoo!! Way to go!!

Celebration is mandatory and it gets easier and becomes more natural the more you do it.

Celebrating can be whatever you want but you must do part of it immediately after goal review. It can be a celebration dance you do right where you are, giving yourself congratulations and a high five in the mirror or, if you're like me, giving yourself some unicorn stickers at the bottom of the goals you just reviewed. All of these can be done immediately.

Next, you are going to give yourself a reward for that week. Make it something you enjoy. It could be 30 minutes reading with a cup of tea, trying a new spot for an outing or giving yourself an extra hour of something you enjoy. One of my favorite rewards is putting away a certain amount of money for something I want that's a luxury for me, but attainable within a few months. Right now I'm high-fiving myself and enjoying my unicorn stickers with a celebratory dance in the moment and putting away some money each week for a piece of jewelry.

Find what works for you and make sure it is sustainable. You know what motivates you. This is not the time for deprivation thinking. Consider what you truly want and enjoy.

Each week at your weekly check-in, you will celebrate and reward yourself. You do these <u>no matter how the three parts before it went</u>. Do not reward yourself more when you achieve all three goals and reward yourself less when some goals are unmet. You reward yourself because you are showing up and completing the check-in. If your week had some challenges and the goals are moved to the next week, that's fine.

We celebrate that we are doing the check-in and forming this habit. If your goals do shift to the next week, you will still have the insight of what happened the week before. Were the goals unrealistic or did you forget a factor that influenced your week? Maybe you're getting better each week at detangling the coming energy and you're riding out the end of that wave. It all gives you information to make decisions for the next week. <u>You may need to celebrate even more because a part of you feels like beating yourself up.</u>

Remember you have resources like the other steps in this program. There is vast help available to you for this, both embodied and inorganic. You don't have to do it alone. Orient to your heart space, ask to be shown your next steps and celebrate your own willingness to make this change. You are doing it!

We celebrate, celebrate, celebrate! Dance around. Write yourself a love letter and mail it to yourself. Make a list of all the ways you are awesome and tape it to your refrigerator. Sing your favorite song to yourself. Give yourself a hug. Tell that amazing soul in the mirror just how wonderful they are and how proud you are of them. Yay you!

Before we end this chapter, I'd like to mention why weekly check-ins are part of the program. First, it is an opportunity to exercise honesty, open mindedness, and willingness which you'll hear more about in later chapters. As with many aspects of this program, you develop personal integrity, accountability and responsibility. It allows us to see ourselves accurately as we look back on our week. It brings us back to our heart space with no intention, other than curiosity. We reaffirm our commitment and love to ourselves. It gives us a way to integrate our program into our daily life.

It also addresses a need that I've seen in myself and in working with others. We have vast inner worlds. We live in bodies spending most of our days interacting with the outside world. It can be easy to spend a day, or two, or a week, pondering or examining our feelings and staying inside our own mind. I found myself here many times. It's beneficial for the type of inner work many of us do. Then when I found out who I truly am, and why I am here, I needed another way to anchor myself in day-to-day life to begin setting pieces in motion for what I am creating. I needed a way to begin moving forward and monitoring my progress and goals so I could look back and see how far I'd come.

Thus, the weekly check-in. It's an anchoring point you will develop as your own path unfolds. It grounds you in the world in which you are called to share your work. It also cuts short those thought loops that keep us focused solely on the mental plane. It helps engage hearts and hands in the world.

You have your starting point now. Over time your check-in will change. This tool is a framework and there is so much available to you here, including what will develop during that time in your heart space. Stay honest, open-minded and willing. What unfolds is magical.

Create Energetic Boundaries with Integrity and Character Building

This is the tool that many I've worked with say is the most challenging… and the most rewarding. I've had people ask if we can skip parts of this chapter. (Nope. Sorry!) People tell me that they don't need to develop personal integrity because they've been doing shadow work for a long time. (Also, no. This typically results in identifying as a "good person" and making things that need to be "addressed" into your shadow. If you continually think that you are a "good" person, you keep yourself from embracing the wholeness of who you truly are as All That Is.)

I used to think it would be great if there were a shortcut to becoming who you were meant to be. But I've done enough of my own exploring, and worked with enough people to find out that there are no substitutes for the gains and satisfaction that come with walking yourself through becoming your own person. The process of finding what is truly important to you and what you want to be representative of your character cannot be rushed. It influences your energetic nature, what you resonate with and the types of beings, both embodied and discarnate, that you interact with.

But first, it's necessary for me to point out one of the biggest traps for people going through spiritual awakening. I call it the Belief System Battle. The players are different depending on which spiritual tradition or background a seeker ascribes to but the mechanism is the same.

Seekers become attached to particular belief systems or explanations. This happens for a variety of reasons. Then the seeker self-limits information, personal contacts and experiences and openness to new ideas by testing what's encountered against this preferred belief system or explanation. If the new input is congruent (or doesn't directly threaten the belief in the preferred belief system), it is accepted. If the new input challenges the preferred belief system, it is rejected and often attacked. It becomes a threat to the comfort and security of the ego and/or the preferred belief system. You see this frequently in online spaces where people debate the "best" ways to be, do or have an experience. What works for one person is shared but it doesn't work for another or is seen as threatening a belief which someone else holds so the speaker and/or the practice is attacked.

For example, let's say a seeker has found an explanation for energy centers in the body or a specific method of awakening practices belonging to a particular branch of a spiritual tradition to be very important in their life. It could be different branches of Buddhism, mystic Christianity, new age practices, indigenous traditions of different locales, different types of magickal practices, Toltec mysticism, theosophic inquiry, etc. The list can go on. The seeker begins limiting their own experiences and interactions to ones that don't challenge what they believe to be valid.

By reducing what is acceptable, they have now begun operating on a smaller field. They have contracted their own awareness for the sake of comfort. The end result of this is ultimately that they diminish their own experience and awakening. Their ability to access new information and to hold seemingly opposing thoughts concurrently is diminished.

This also creates division within spiritual communities. The old adage, "If you aren't for me, you're against me" comes to mind. The totality of who we are as All That Is becomes lost. The seeker loses sight of the multiplicity of paths to Source. It's one thing to develop friendships. It's another to discount someone because of their experience, outlook or practices.

So why do we become so attached to our ideas of how things are that we can't examine new information?

How did this begin?

What are the risks?

We become attached for a variety of reasons. I'll provide a few, but honest examination of your own life will show you more.

We become attached to certain spiritual belief systems because they were helpful to us at one point. We may become attached because someone we trust told us something was true. We may take on belief systems that fit well with belief systems and explanations that our ego already believes to be true. We may become attached to belief systems and practices because we believe it will get us something we want or because it worked for someone else. We may take on belief systems that feed our ego and tell us something we want to be true about ourselves. We may become attached to belief systems that explain something we haven't been able to explain and are desperate to understand with our thinking mind. This list goes on.

There are two main risks. The first is that you do not accomplish what you came here to do. The second is that you do not refine yourself enough to move on to the next level and repeat another incarnation. (This is not a punishment. It is simply repeating a choice to gain more experience. Ultimately, it is all happening in the same one moment so it is simply another incarnation. If you want this to be your last incarnation in this realm, you will need to master this.)

These risks are possible because you have narrowed what ideas and experiences you will entertain. You become unable to examine any new experiences or information with curiosity. Your awakening stymies. You cannot assimilate new input or broaden your consciousness to an understanding that can hold seemingly opposing viewpoints and paradoxes.

Unfortunately, this is the most common impediment to spiritual development I see. It keeps seekers from diverse backgrounds with complementary experiences from interacting and working together. I see it keep seekers from following up on insights and intuitions because the preferred belief system doesn't match with the inspired action. The seeker chooses the preferred belief system instead of curiosity and exploration in following their inspiration. The inspired action is not taken and an opportunity for expansion is missed. (Note: There will be more opportunities but there is a long term detrimental effect here. However, this book is not the place for that explanation.)

This chapter is about developing personal integrity and character formation. Why am I talking about the Belief System Battle? What does that have to do with personal integrity?

You need to know about the Belief System Battle because it is the biggest impediment to developing personal integrity. You need to be able to recognize it in yourself and others. Once you know about the Belief System Battle, it's fairly easy to identify. Often, interactions with a new person are driven by the other person's inquiry about your belief systems and experiences to see if they match. You are testing each other out to see if it is safe to continue, to see if you both agree on some core premise. Once the other person feels that their belief system is safe with you, they can explore other topics of conversation. If there isn't any common ground around belief systems, the interaction typically ends for seekers caught in the Belief System Battle. The opportunity for expansion and a new experience is missed.

But once you are aware of this dynamic at play or you are confident in your own identity, it's possible to have another scenario. Instead of discussing belief systems and experiences and looking for a match, you have many more options. When meeting a new person or experience, you can follow your intuition or inner guidance. Maybe you feel like you need to introduce yourself to someone across the room. Perhaps your eye is drawn to something on their shirt and you ask about it. It ends up being exactly what you needed next in your journey. Or you ask some questions about the other person. Getting to know him or her will reveal more topics that may pique your interest. Of course, you may not be called to interact with a person at all. You may feel pulled to enter a garden at a party and begin stacking rocks. Then it attracts the attention of the only person at the party you really need to speak with. Stay open to ideas. There's more to explore here but the point is that opting out of the Belief System Battle is an option that can become more familiar to you over time. It has great rewards. You meet some amazing people and have great experiences and stories to tell!

So, now you know how to identify the Belief System Battle. It sidelines your awakening, just like shadow work does. It also hinders developing personal integrity because you become focused on matching your belief system to outside input rather than developing yourself. When you are focused on developing yourself and becoming a person of integrity, the focus moves from being right to being coherent with your own values. You become willing to be wrong if it helps you become honest and whole. You recognize that you have an ego that wants to be right and you don't let it run the show.

So the next question is, Why do I need to develop personal integrity?

You need to develop personal integrity because you want who you are as an energetic being to be driving your awakening, not attachment to belief systems. This matters because you want to develop your intuition and psychic skills for guidance, not to be reliant on outside input. The non-cognitive information you receive as guidance, whether it's a hunch, your clairaudience or a dream, is influenced by what you have decided is important to you. If you decide that a certain belief system is important, you will receive guidance pertinent to that belief system. If you decide that someone has wronged you, you will receive guidance pertinent to that interaction. If you decide that you want to become a being of integrity and learn truth even if it shows your belief systems to be wrong, you will receive guidance of a higher quality which broadens your consciousness and expands your mental capacity for understanding.

This alignment with personal integrity has additional benefits. First, this focus on personal integrity gives the thinking mind something to focus on besides particular belief systems and reinforcing those belief systems. It reduces the ego's dependency on being right or being seen as superior. Second, it strongly influences which energies and entities you encounter as guides and in your experience. As you set a higher goal, you attract beings and energies aligned with that goal among others. In short, if you want higher truth, choose that above all else and your inspiration and intuitions will begin to match it.

This is also a starting point for communication with other beings that value integrity and truth. There are great benefits when you become proficient at interacting with inorganic beings (or spirits) as well, but that is beyond the scope of this book. Suffice it to say, you will have a foundation with this program as your starting point.

Now, we need a unicorn.

Just need to drop one here. That was a lot of info.

Feel free to break out some crayons. Every chapter needs at least one unicorn or funny picture. That's a rule. I made it up, just now. I don't know why but I'm making it a rule. We are here to have a good time after all! Even if a little work comes our way.

Say hi to Smooni.

Smooni loves to brighten days and eat ice cream. She's pretty much the best friend of five year olds everywhere.

OK, Smooni. Thanks for stopping in. Catch you later, Beautiful. We're building personal integrity here.

Back to business.

What is personal integrity? How do we develop personal integrity?

My definition of personal integrity is the process of becoming aligned with the values that you hold. Exactly what that looks like will vary from person to person. You need to be clear on what you value as you develop a personal code of values for yourself. And you need to understand that my definition says "becoming." There is no arrival point. As in life, we are in a continual process of becoming who we desire to be. Personal integrity for me means that I am someone who keeps her word, is present for what shows up in life and relationships, contributes to help others and cares for herself.

Now, I'm not perfect at this. I simply do my best each day. Having personal integrity means you strive to become the kind of person that you want to interact with and enjoy being around. One of the biggest markers is whether you act the same in front of others as you do when you're alone. Being able to be in coherence with your own values when no one is watching is a big deal. Because ultimately, the only person who will ever know if you have lived up to what you set out to do is you. But your energetic signature will display it as well for those who can read it.

The core of personal integrity lies in what you are focused on. In this program it is a concentration on H.O.W. This is a concept put forward in the big book of Alcoholics Anonymous. It may be mentioned in other places, but 12 step rooms were my introduction to it. It stands for honesty, open mindedness, and willingness. These principles have changed my life. I know they will change yours.

My personal favorite is willingness, because in those times when I am not ready to be as honest or as open minded as I'd like, I can always be willing. If I'm having a difficulty, I ask for the willingness to be willing so I can be or embody whatever change I'm looking to make. That softens my resistance, and I can be kind with myself, while still focusing on what my next steps are.

Being honest, open minded and willing is a full-time job. I suggest you go easy on yourself and be sweet to you. As we develop personal integrity, we also foster a commitment to personal growth. As you'll discover, developing integrity is ultimately about relationship – relating to others, relating to ourselves, relating to our environment and the decisions and values surrounding those relationships.

We learn to focus on doing our best. With that commitment, we recognize that our best will vary. Some days we are capable of fulfilling our obligations and vision for the day. Some days we are not. Through using the rest of the tools in this program, and being honest, open minded, and willing, we cultivate self-reflection. This allows us to see ourselves clearly to know when we need to challenge ourselves, and when we need to step back and regroup. This insight comes with time and willingness. Remember to be kind to yourself.

There is no race. The journey has no end. And we have multiple helpers along the way, so we are not doing the heavy lifting ourselves.

The foundation of this tool is reliant on learning how you want to approach and interact with your emotions. I find this is the biggest stumbling block to developing integrity. Emotions are non-cognitive information. There are entire books and systems of thinking around how to interact with emotions. I would love to add an entire list of processes and methods of approach here. My source told me no. This program is made to be customizable. The beautiful people who are brave enough to open themselves to working with me have shown me that there are many, many ways to approach this. Personally, I have seven different approaches I use for myself. I use whichever I feel would fit in the moment. Over the past 20 years, I've used over four dozen different methods of addressing emotions. It's important to try new things so that you can synthesize and create methods that work for you as you evolve.

Use whatever methods you like. Make sure that the method doesn't judge emotions and sees them as valuable information. We know joy feels better than resentment, but all emotions give you information and are valid. I've learned some of my most important and necessary lessons while experiencing fear. Then I learned how to ask for a more enjoyable, learning experience, and what the fear was indicating that I needed to address. We are not abdicating responsibility for emotions and we are not denying emotions that don't feel as pleasurable as others. We need them all.

Tip: **Stay out of the ER**. As we learn which methods we prefer, we remind ourselves to stay out of the ER. The ER stands for Expectations and Resentments. Both of these place our personal power in someone else's control. Reclaiming agency and personal accountability in our lives is a big portion of personal integrity and feels much better.

Meetings as Points of Action to Solidify Your Transformation

Meetings are the cornerstone to solidify your transformation. This is where we separate out those people who want to read this book to see if they agree with it, try out a few ideas, and when they don't get the change they're looking for, put the book on the shelf or give it away. They tell themselves, "This program doesn't work, just like all the others." Then they go looking for the next thing. That's fine. This program isn't for everyone. It's for people who want change and are willing to walk a heart-centered path with others to do it.

If I had to pick only one of these chapters to implement right away to get started, this is the one. I love this entire program, and all these steps work together in a very mystifying, yet satisfying way. You will eventually be using all these steps to achieve the transformation and revelation you're looking for.

But if you can only do one to start, this would be it. Attending and participating in a meeting is the best step to start if you can only do one step. You can attend one of our meetings, meet other people working this program, say hi and get as involved as you'd like. You can also attend a meeting, say nothing and take in what we have to offer.

People who regularly attend and participate in meetings get vastly better results with this program than those who don't. I deliberately formed this program around meetings, because they are so transformational. I'll be honest; I don't have much confidence in long-term transformation without regular meeting attendance. While I'm a mystic at heart, and have experienced multiple miracles in my life, I don't believe you will have the same powerful change in your life if you don't participate in meetings while establishing and personalizing your program. But I am happy to be wrong. I want this program to help as many people as possible in as many ways as it can be made available.

I made meetings the foundation of this program for several reasons. First, attending a meeting - showing up to a room full of strangers and identifying that you are ready for something more in your life - is a powerful action.

That's one of the things this program relies on - action. Being willing and taking this first step separates you. It separates you from everyone else who reads this book and says, "I'll try this some other time. I am too busy right now." It is the people willing to take action who will realize the totality of who they are and why they're here through this program. As I learned in the rooms of my recovery - Meeting makers make it. You know that you will need to make this a priority. It's sending a message to the cosmos that you are ready for more and engaged in your own awakening. You resolve waiting and put things into motion.

Ready to make this a priority? Take two minutes to visit my website and make contact to find out when meetings are. It's below.

Go ahead. I'll wait.

QueenHeterodoxika.com

All done?   Excellent!

I'm excited to see you at the next meeting! Sweet!

(I think a unicorn snuck in while you went to the website. No worries; they are friendly.)

Why else did I make meetings so important? Glad you asked!

As well as cultivating willingness, meetings help dissolve the sense of isolation and loneliness that often accompanies spiritual awakening and spiritual work. I often hear from people who wished they had found me and my work sooner. They felt alone and isolated for most of their lives, unable to discuss much of what goes on in their interior world.

I also know exactly what this is like. I found spiritual groups during my awakening but they were always built around subscribing to a particular belief system and some were built around entrepreneurs building a following and charged an exorbitant fee. It is common to feel lonely whether going through a dark night of the soul or not. Sometimes you just want to be able to share something that you're going through and be seen and heard. That's something, increasingly rare currently, but so necessary for walking this path. Sharing at meetings and supporting others at meetings builds what is necessary for sustainability on what is sometimes a challenging path. It builds community and belonging. We are united in the common goal of becoming who we were meant to be and we are supportive of each other and our diverse paths.

Community! Togetherness! Sis-boom-bah! Yaaaayyy! Meetings!!!

(Have I mentioned that I love teamwork!?)

What else are meetings good for?

What?!

There's more? Really?

Yes. I will give you more reasons meetings are awesome.

Remember that chapter on personal integrity? Guess where you can start practicing all those skills right away?

Your next meeting!

Yes, you too can practice all these and more!

Honesty! Open mindedness! Willingness! Personal accountability!

That personal code of conduct you've been working on?

Time to practice. Time to share.

When it comes down to it, it's just interpersonal skills. It's how you interact with yourself and how you interact with others. Meetings are a relatively easy way to start because meetings have a set format. Once you've been to a few, you have a good idea of when people talk, what the expectations and roles are, and how to interact. Also, you can meet new people.

What a bonus! It's a great way to keep our program front and center to reinforce what we are practicing.

Before you ask, there is one more reason I absolutely adore meetings. This reason is integral to this program. I don't want to give away too much. (HINT: It's the next chapter.) Not only do meetings allow us to practice building integrity but... stay with me here, it's better than you think... Meetings are your gateway to...

Service!

It's easier than you think. I promise! Doesn't hurt at all! Actually, if you are reading this and you can talk, then you can do service. Meet me in the next chapter. I'll tell you how easy it is and how it's going to help you.

Come on….. Grab a snack. I'll bring the unicorns.

We got this. We're almost done.

Service Connects You to Others

Hello! Welcome to our final chapter.

Feeling good? Did you bring a snack for yourself?

Great!

I told you in the last chapter that the final reason meetings are beneficial is due to service.

So, what is service?

Do you have to do manual labor?

Tell your neighbors about this program and spread the word?

Am I trying to start an MLM empire?

Nope.

Nothing like that. I actually designed everything in the program to be free so it's accessible to as many people who want it as possible. I do charge to work with me personally and I'm feeling a community membership coming for additional support but you never need to those to take full advantage of this program. Everything you need to be successful is found in the program in this book. Your willingness to apply it is the only hurdle.

You need to go to a meeting.

And read.

Out loud. So other people can hear you.

It's two paragraphs. Can you do that?

Of course you can!

So this chapter doesn't feel so scary anymore, does it?

You can go to a meeting and read. Now you've done some service. Way to work your program! Woohoo!!

Great job!

So, what is service and why is it in this program?

Service is any activity done for the benefit of others with a heart willing to help while respecting free will. It starts at meetings and we move it outward as we are inspired.

Meetings are a great place to do service because it strengthens our fellowship. It makes us all responsible for ensuring the meeting runs smoothly.

There are always opportunities for service at a meeting - doing a reading, using the timer for shares, speaking with newcomers after the meeting and signing up to lead an upcoming meeting. Not only does it help the group, but it keeps you connected and engaged as well. As with all the steps in this program, how you practice service will change over time as your intuition and personal guidance evolve.

Not bad in exchange for some reading, right? You got this.

Congratulations! We're done here. Now your action begins and you take this into daily life.

You've read this manual. You know why shadow work doesn't work once awakening starts. You have tools and you're on the meeting list.

I'm excited for you. Your life is about to level up. I know what's in you which is why I created this program. You possess amazing potential that needs to be seen and shared.

Don't worry. This isn't goodbye. You know where to find me online and I'll see you at the next meeting.

Further Resources

Congratulations!

You've finished the book.

I have further resources I'm developing to support the program. I'll be releasing videos, worksheets, opportunities for online sharing and whatever Source moves me to share and create. You'll find those on my website and social media accounts.

Website: QueenHeterodoxika.com

X (formerly Twitter): @YourAuntieQueen

More social media coming soon. My website is the best place for updates. Find out about meetings and more there. You'll get updates of future meetings and all additional resources as they are released. See you at a meeting soon!